Born Again:
Not Just For Heaven

Flying Eagle Publications

Flying Eagle Publications

We endeavor to create materials that encourage and strengthen you in your journey through life. It is also our aim to equip believers so that they can reach farther dream larger and get their message heard. The eagle flies closest to the Creator and bears His message to all. That is our hope too. That is why we do what we do– to teach, entertain and inspire.

Born Again:

Not Just For Heaven

Flying Eagle Publications

Unless otherwise noted, all scripture taken from the King James Version of the Bible. Scriptures marked KJV are taken from the KING JAMES VERSION (KJV): KING JAMES VERSION, public domain.

Scriptures marked CEV are taken from the CONTEMPORARY ENGLISH VERSION (CEV):Scripture taken from the CONTEMPORARY ENGLISH VERSION copyright© 1995 by the American Bible Society. Used by permission.

Scriptures marked GNB are from the Good News Bible © 1994 published by the Bible Societies/HarperCollins Publishers Ltd UK, Good News Bible© American Bible Society 1966, 1971, 1976, 1992. Used with permission.

Scripture taken from the Literal Translation of the Holy Bible Copyright © 1976 - 2000
By Jay P. Green, Sr.
Used by permission of the copyright holder.

Scriptures marked MKJV are taken from the MODERN KING JAMES VERSION (MKJV):
Scripture taken from the Holy Bible, MODERN KING JAMES VERSION copyright© 1962 —1998 by Jay P. Green, Sr. Used by permission of the copyright holder.

Born Again: Not Just For Heaven
Print ISBN: 978-1-7327688-3-3
Editors: Dee Farrell and Benjamin Emrick

Copyright ©Flying Eagle Publications 2020.
Flyingeaglepublications.com
Cover image by Ian Espinosa courtesy of Unsplash.
Design by Haley Jula.

All Rights Reserved under International Copyright Law. No part of this book may be reproduced or transmitted in any form or by any means.

Printed in the United States.

First...

Welcome to our Foundations of the Faith series of books. In this particular teaching, you will learn about the term born again, when it was first used, what it means and why it is an important step to take to become a follower of Jesus.

If you type the words born again into Google's search bar, a few options appear in the list box of related searches. There is born again church, born again in the Bible, what does it mean to be born again of water and spirit, born again what does it really mean, and the danger of born again Christianity.

Wikipedia even has an entry on born again.

It is important to understand there may be a difference between the concept of an evangelical and a person who says they are born again. The terms born again and evangelical are not necessarily interchangeable.

In 2017 LifeWay Research conducted a survey in which they separated the terms and asked people to identify as one or the other. There were some surprising results. 24% of Americans identified as evangelical but only 15% had evangelical beliefs. What should an evangelical believe? The study listed four main beliefs:

- the Bible is the highest authority
- Jesus' death on the cross is the only way to remove the penalty for a person's sins
- Jesus is the only way to gain eternal life in heaven
- it is important to tell others about Jesus

But only 15% of the people identifying as evangelicals in the study actually held those beliefs. Barna conducted a similar survey and found only 6% of Americans to be true evangelicals.

Also, the traditional political image of an evangelical did not match what the study revealed. LifeWay found 4 in 10 evangelicals were not white. Barna's study discovered of American evangelicals 16% identified as black and 11% Hispanic. The conclusion is an evangelical may not believe what you think they should or look like you think they should.

So what about the people in the study choosing the description born again over evangelical?

In LifeWay's study 29% identified as born again, and 30% of that group were more likely to agree with evangelical beliefs and identify as black.

But for either group, whether born again or evangelical, less than half would actually agree with what the Bible states a follower of Jesus should believe and how they should behave.

That is why you can't rely on your coworker or friend to be your example of what born again means. Obviously most born again Christians do not understand it. Instead, it is necessary to go to the source of the definition, the origin of the concept, which is in the Bible in the book of John.

With that in mind let's begin our study of born again, the biblical version.

Chapter 1

Nicodemus

Man is a spirit, the Bible shows us, and the world was created for him. It is a different picture than the world draws for man. Evolution is concerned with man's chemicals and particles and atoms. Education is focused on the brain; medicine, man's bodily systems, and so on for the rest of his affairs.

The world uses an outside in approach. Man's Creator, however, reveals the correct method for man's dealings is the opposite: from the inside—spirit— out. But ah, we are getting ahead of ourselves...

The book of John is the first to mention the term born again. The book is part of the New Testament called the Gospels or good tidings. This "good" message refers to the fulfillment of an agreement God made with Adam and Abraham. We will be learning more about the agreement later.

In the Old Testament God said He would bless those who followed Him. This promise was included in His agreement with Abraham in Genesis 12. God's agreements are called covenants in the Bible.

Understanding God's covenants is the key to understanding the Old Testament and God's "wrath" as it is called. Understanding them is also key to knowing what Jesus' death on the cross means for you and how it benefits you on earth and later in heaven.

After the Israelites had left Egypt, God gave them a detailed system of laws and religious practices. This system was the standard God used for forgiving sin and for the blessings He promised. It continued the practice of animal sacrifice which they had used in the past to worship God. The law was the method God used for teaching right from wrong.

But in the New Testament God revealed a "new" standard. It wasn't fully understood, however, until the apostle Paul began teaching it. He realized Jesus died on our behalf (Romans 5-8), as a substitute.

No longer would animal sacrifices be required to pay for sins because Jesus as God's Son had taken it upon Himself to die once for all men. A new era had begun with the death and resurrection of Jesus.

You might think God's new agreement or what is called the New Testament began with the birth of Jesus. While His birth is certainly our introduction to the New Testament accounts, the agreement went into effect when Jesus rose from the dead and the Holy Spirit arrived in Acts 2. In God's mind it was established in Genesis 3 that Jesus was coming to earth. But while He walked the earth, Jesus lived under the Old Testament covenants. He began to introduce mankind to what He called the kingdom during His ministry.

Hebrews 9 compares the first system of animal sacrifice with Jesus' death and says in verse fifteen that Jesus became the mediator of the new testament. The word translated new is the Greek word *kainos* (kigh-NAHS) which means fresh, new. Testament is *diathēkē* (deeahTHAYkay), meaning a contract, arrangement or covenant. The New Testament was the coming of a fresh arrangement or covenant between God and all the people on earth, not just the Israelites as Paul would later realize.

When Jesus first used the words born again, He was talking to a man who understood the Old Covenant system. But he, like everyone else at the time, was ignorant of Jesus' real purpose. What he learned stunned him.

The author of the book of John was, as you might have guessed, a man named John. John was a young man when he first became a follower of Jesus. Later, he wrote down the events he saw during the three and a half years he traveled with Him. He wrote four other books too, three other books called John and labeled 1, 2, and 3 and another book named Revelation.

In the book of John, plain old John also called the Gospel of John, he documented a meeting between Jesus and a man named Nicodemus. John must have been present during their conversation, and perhaps there were other of Jesus' disciples present also. John wrote:

> There was a man of the Pharisees, named Nicodemus, a ruler of the Jews:

> The same came to Jesus by night, and said unto him, Rabbi, we know that thou art a teacher come from God: for no man can do these miracles that thou doest, except God be with him.
>
> John 3:1-2

If you read John's gospel from the beginning, you may not connect the events in chapter two with this meeting because John didn't write his book in chapters. The Bible editors did that. But in John 2:23 we are told Jesus and his disciples were in Jerusalem for the Passover. "And as He was in Jerusalem at the Passover, at the feast, many believed in His name when they saw the miracles which He did."

Nicodemus must have seen these miracles as we will see later. But the events in chapter two reveal an incident Nicodemus was surely aware of. While he was in Jerusalem for the Passover, Jesus visited the Temple and saw a type of market set up in the place where the Gentiles were supposed to be able to worship God.

Gentiles are people who are not Jewish. Some Gentiles admired Israel's God and God accepted them even though they were not Israelites. If they wanted to worship the Jewish God, Yahweh, they could only do so in that specific place of the Temple.

But this market was running in that location, and the Gentiles' right to worship wasn't being respected. So Jesus made a whip and drove out the cattle and sheep. It was quite a spectacle, and the priests who had violated the traditional rules and allowed the merchants to set up there demanded to know who gave Jesus the authority to do that.

Nicodemus surely heard about this or saw it himself because Nicodemus was a Pharisee. He might have been one of the ones questioning Jesus. A Pharisee is the Greek *Pharisaios* (fahdreSIGHus) and related to the Hebrew word *parash* (pahdrRash). It means a separatist, exclusively religious, to make distinct, to distinguish. According to Bible scholar Rick Renner, this means they viewed themselves separated by God for His purposes; thus, they were extremely committed and even fanatical in their service to God.

Nicodemus was also a ruler in the Sanhedrin, and in John's description of him the word for ruler means first rank magistrate. This made him an important man in the local synagogue, and by that we know he was rich and influential.

It is in John 7:50 we are told Nicodemus was a member of the Sanhedrin which was the ruling body making up the Jewish court system. We are not told why he came to Jesus at night. The Sanhedrin judged accused lawbreakers during the day. Is this why Nicodemus came to Jesus at night? Because they were both busy during the day?

But the court did not meet on festival days. Was it because Nicodemus' presence could have caused Jesus more trouble from the Pharisees? Perhaps he wanted to talk with Jesus privately and both men were important and apt to draw crowds of admirers?

Born Again: Not Just For Heaven

We cannot be sure of his reasons for coming to Jesus at night, but it seems the visit was motivated by his curiosity in Jesus and fear of his colleagues. They did not appreciate Jesus' disruption at the Temple. Jesus never rebuked Nicodemus for his oddly timed visit. He didn't seem to mind the interruption. It was a quiet time of day, and Nicodemus could focus on His words, not the priests'. Jesus must have been pleased with Nicodemus' interest.

Jesus was consistently approachable and willing to serve, a quality that set Him apart from most important men of His day. Despite being hungry or tired, He turned no one away, including Nicodemus.

And here we should realize the two men had some things in common. For example, both lived morally and both believed in the resurrection. Both respected and honored God's word given to the prophets, in the Psalms and Proverbs, in the books of history and the law. They could have discussed many things, but Nicodemus wasn't interested in talking shop exactly. This visit was personal.

Nicodemus began the conversation. "Rabbi, we know that You have come as a teacher from God." (John 3:2) John 1:38 tells us the title rabbi meant Teacher. "Rabbi (which being translated is called Teacher)."

Its original meaning also contained the idea of great or distinguished. The word was used like Master, a term designating great learning and respect like a PhD today. It was a title the Pharisees used for themselves. Nicodemus addressed Jesus with the highest respect he knew. He humbled himself as much as he understood. He thought Jesus was sent by God. He didn't know Jesus was God...yet.

At other times the Pharisees came to Jesus in a group and interrupted His teaching. They were always questioning Jesus about His authority like when they asked in Luke 20, "Tell us by what authority you do these things, or who is it who gave to you this authority?"

Jesus wasn't a graduate from their so-called rabbi schools. His habit of outsmarting them and knowing more than they did always drew their ire. But Nicodemus didn't doubt Jesus deserved the title of rabbi.

Nicodemus must have been one of the Pharisees listening to Jesus teach because he wouldn't have given Him the title of Master Teacher or Master Theologian lightly. Nicodemus said, "...we know that You have come as a teacher from God."

Who was he talking about when he said we? Surely not the group of Jerusalem priests? Most of them would have never admitted such a thing. Perhaps Nicodemus was just being gracious.

But Joseph of Arimathea was also a member of the Sanhedrin. He was the one who asked Pilate for permission to take Jesus' body after the crucifixion. John called him a follower of Jesus but a secret follower because he feared the Jews.

And we are back to the fact that Nicodemus may have come at night because he too feared his fellow priests and coworkers. We also know Nicodemus and Joseph knew each other because together they prepared Jesus' body for burial. Perhaps he was referring to Joseph?

But the reference to "we" may have addressed and included the disciples sitting with Jesus as most certainly one of them was John. Or just John, because later at Jesus' trial in the Sanhedrin, John gained entry because he knew the high priest. (John 18:15) He may have been acquainted with Nicodemus as well.

The point is Nicodemus was not being falsely gracious to Jesus when he said "we" know. There were others, either present or whom he knew, that realized Jesus deserved the title of rabbi.

Nicodemus said, "...for no man can do these miracles which you do unless God is with him." So we know by this verse he must have seen the miracles Jesus did in John 2:23. "And as He was in Jerusalem at the Passover, at the feast, many believed in His name when they saw the miracles which He did."

Or, Nicodemus saw the evidence of those miracles such as the person who was blind or deaf or was lame or sick, but then they weren't.

To Nicodemus, Jesus' arrival in Jerusalem and His ministry there was astounding. It impressed him so much, he wanted to know more but he didn't really know how to go about asking.

His heart was seeking the truth, but his position in Jerusalem made his honest search risky to his reputation. He obviously didn't share his fellow priests' indignation of Jesus. But he didn't know what to make of this young rabbi either.

So he came by night and, in the humility he knew to offer, sat with this incredible man who had caught his attention and wonder. Perhaps he didn't even know what to ask or what he was really searching for, but Jesus as the Word who became flesh as John said in 1:14, was about to pierce between joint and marrow to the root of Nicodemus' questions.

We'll take a look at that conversation in the next chapter.

Going Deeper

Who was Nicodemus?

Describe God's covenants.

Did Jesus live subject to the Old Testament covenant? Explain.

Compare the old covenant with The New Testament. What changed?

Why did Jesus drive livestock out of the Temple?

Do you think society takes for granted that credentials equal knowledge? Explain.

Do you rely more on the opinions of pastors and teachers or what the Bible says? Is one more important than the other? Why or why not?

Get quiet and ask God what He would like you to learn as you read this book.

Chapter 2

The Conversation

John began his gospel by describing Jesus as the Word and declaring Him to be God. Psalm 107:20 also points to Jesus as the Word. It says, "He [God] sent His Word and healed them."

Hebrews 4:12 shows us another way the word works. "For the word of God is quick, and powerful, and sharper than any twoedged sword, piercing even to the dividing asunder of soul and spirit, and of the joints and marrow, and is a discerner of the thoughts and intents of the heart." Nicodemus was about to experience this aspect of the word in his conversation with Jesus.

After Nicodemus' gracious opening, Jesus quickly got to the root of his problem. John 3:3 says, "Jesus answered and said unto him, Verily, verily, I say unto thee, Except a man be born again, he cannot see the kingdom of God."

It is interesting that it says Jesus answered. Nicodemus hadn't asked any questions yet. It would seem an odd response, off topic, if we didn't understand that Jesus was able to pierce and divide down to the spirit and soul of Nicodemus and discern the thoughts and intent of his heart. And in this sentence Jesus revealed what Nicodemus was seeking.

Nicodemus wanted to see, *eidō* (EYEdoh), also meaning to know or to understand the kingdom of God. Nicodemus was a priest, a master teacher himself, but he never healed anyone. He didn't teach with the authority Jesus did.

In case you didn't know, it was noted by the Jews that Jesus was different from their teachers of the law. They said Jesus taught with authority. (Matt. 7:29) Their teachers contradicted each other's doctrines, much like Bible scholars today, and they must not have been able to give definitive answers to the people's questions. Jesus could, and He did.

And so, Nicodemus was wondering what does this guy know that I don't? What does he have that I haven't? How can I know and do these things? But Jesus' response only created more questions.

This is the first instance of the term born again used in the Bible. Born is *gennaō* (genNAHoh), meaning to beget, bring forth, be delivered, bear, generation or regeneration. The same translation is used in Matthew's genealogy list, and since Jewish priests were familiar with Old Testament genealogies, Nicodemus knew what Jesus meant.

Gennaō is also the word used to describe Jesus' physical birth and John the Baptist's. It carries the meaning of continuing the family position (authority), generation or regeneration. And, according to *The New International Dictionary of New Testament Theology*, it is used here in John in relation to the origins of the believer. The believer is brought forth or generated.

Again is *anōthen* (AHNohthen). It has a double meaning, from above and from the first as in anew. Putting the meanings of *gennaō* and *anōthen* together, what Jesus was saying was if Nicodemus wanted to experience the kingdom of God, he would need to be regenerated or reborn from above to continue a family position of authority.

Nicodemus was astounded. How could a man go back into his mother's womb? But Nicodemus was focused on what the Bible calls flesh or carnal knowledge. Jesus wasn't talking about Nicodemus' body. He was talking about his spirit, and this rebirth was to be accomplished from above, not by an earthly process.

Nicodemus got hung up on the born again idea, and he missed what Jesus was saying. He wasn't going to understand everything he wanted to know until he was born again because then he would be able to see— *eidō*.

Perhaps this makes it clear to you why some people misinterpret Bible verses or do not understand their clear meaning. You can't take in God's truth with just your mind and understand it. It is spiritually recognized as it says in 1Corinthians 2:14. "But the natural man does not receive the things of the Spirit of God, for they are foolishness to him; neither can he know them, because they are spiritually discerned." (MKJV)

In His conversation with Nicodemus, Jesus followed with a more in depth explanation. Your Bible translation may say verily verily or surely or for certain. Basically Jesus was saying, "I am telling you the truth. Before you can get into God's kingdom, you must be born not only by water which is a physical birth through your parents, but by the Spirit which is from your heavenly Father."

He said spirit begets spirit. "That which is born of the flesh is flesh; and that which is born of the Spirit is spirit." (John 3:6) He was talking about the Holy Spirit giving a new spirit to man. David prayed for this in Psalm 51 when he asked for a renewed spirit. Renew is the Hebrew word *châdash*, and it means to repair or rebuild.

Nicodemus wanted to know what Jesus knew. Jesus told him it boiled down to seeing or knowing the kingdom. But that required him to be born from above. Something had to change. That something was Nicodemus' spirit.

Nicodemus must have been sitting there in amazement because Jesus told him not to be surprised that a person had to be reborn. But he must have been taking all this in because Jesus continued the lesson. He compared the Holy Spirit with the wind, saying that the wind blows wherever it wants. We can hear the sound and see the effects of the wind, but we do not know where it comes from or where it is going next.

Jesus said it is like that with everyone who is born of the Spirit. You don't see the Spirit; therefore you can't see His coming and going. In Acts 2 He came with a sound of a rushing wind and tongues of fire.

The Conversation

You may see or hear His effects or feel His presence, but you don't see *Him*.

This concept of born from above upended Nicodemus' theology, and it does the same to theologians of our day. All Nicodemus had to say was, "How can this be?" To which Jesus answered, "You are a Master Teacher and you don't know these things?"

The fact is no one understood the truths Jesus taught until after Jesus' resurrection and Acts 2. That is, until they were born again and filled with the Holy Spirit. Not even David understood the fullness of his prayer. Nicodemus certainly went home meditating on Jesus' words and searching the Old Testament Scriptures for revelation. He certainly knew the words of Ezekiel and Isaiah.

> Then will I sprinkle clean water upon you, and ye shall be clean: from all your filthiness, and from all your idols, will I cleanse you. A new heart also will I give you, and a new spirit will I put within you: and I will take away the stony heart out of your flesh, and I will give you an heart of flesh. And I will put my spirit within you, and cause you to walk in my statutes, and ye shall keep my judgments, and do them. (Ezekiel 36:25-27)
>
> For I will pour water upon him that is thirsty, and floods upon the dry ground:

> I will pour my spirit upon thy seed,
> and my blessing upon thine offspring...
> (Isaiah 44:3)

Nicodemus knew the verses. Now he was pondering the truths Jesus had revealed to him in light of them. If he wanted to enter into the kingdom of God, he needed a different spirit, a new heart[1] like it said in Ezekiel. He couldn't get in with the old one. And he would never understand or experience fully how the kingdom worked if he didn't get this different spirit.

But you may be wondering why anyone would need a new spirit? We'll find out in the next chapter.

---

[1] Hebrew writers understood the heart to be the life giving organ of the body and the source for the intellect and emotions. They considered man's spirit to be the energizing force of the heart and that which controlled the intellect. That is why man's heart and spirit are used interchangeably or in parallel in Scripture.

Going Deeper

What did Nicodemus want to see?

Define born again.

Why does being born again make you better able to understand the Bible?

What is something about the concept of born again that is new to you?

Ask God to reveal any part of the meaning that you may be missing or misunderstanding. Write down what He shows you.

Chapter 3

Why We Need to be Born Again

In the last chapter we learned what born again means, born from above, and that it is the spirit of a man that needs to have a rebirth through the Spirit of God.

But why would God reject our spirits when it is He who formed us? What is wrong with man's spirit that it needs a redo?

To understand this we have to go all the way back to the beginning. To Genesis. You may have heard about the Garden of Eden. Perhaps you think it is a creation myth. Many believe that.

When you read the New Testament, however, you learn Jesus referred to it as fact. In Matthew 19:4 the Pharisees were trying to expose a fault in Jesus' teaching. Instead, Jesus showed their ignorance of Genesis 1, and He asked them if they had read it. Ouch.

Jesus made numerous references to Satan, one of the characters in the Garden account. Jesus taught about the spiritual realm and how it worked; something they knew little about. Hence, the focus on Satan.

Jesus showed His authority over spirits called demons by casting them out of people. He said these spirits had their own ruling system, and Satan was their leader. He also called Satan the god of this world. (John 14:30)

The word for world in John 14 and John 12:31 is *kosmos*, meaning an orderly arrangement. Satan did not create the world, but he is the god of culture in this sense, the music, art, values, etc. It is ordered by his arrangement, and he is embedded and rooted in it. That is why Christians are warned repeatedly not to be immersed in it or love it.

Satan is a Hebrew word meaning opponent. The book of Revelation is Jesus' revelation to John, and it is full of references to Satan. The twelfth chapter is a history lesson of Satan's fight against God and man.

There are very few references to Satan as a person in the Old Testament; most are in the book of Job. The Israelites did not understand their enemy. When Jesus came, He exposed Satan's identity, character and works. John wrote, "He that committeth sin is of the devil; for the devil sinneth from the beginning. For this purpose the Son of God was manifested, that he might destroy the works of the devil." (1John 3:8)

But what are the works of the slanderer, *diabolos* as the Greek renders the word devil? Again, to find out we have to go back to the beginning. Let's learn what really happened in the Garden.

The Garden was perfect God said. It was a park-like setting where growing food was easy and all you had to do was gather your fruits and veggies for supper. Animals were tame, and the weather was always a perfect temperature.

God created this perfect home for man. It was carefully designed to meet all his needs and provide beauty and enjoyment. Man's purpose was equally pleasing. He was created to fellowship with God.

To be able to commune with the Creator of the universe, man would need to share God's characteristics like thought and speech. But God went beyond that. He gave man a spirit and made him in His image.[1]

Perhaps you have heard man was created to be a little lower than angels. In the Bible, however, angels minister to man. (Hebrews 1:14) Some Bibles interpret Psalm 8:5 to say angels, but the Hebrew says *min 'ĕlôhîym*, from or part of God or the Godhead. *Green's Literal Translation* says, "You have made him lack a little from God."

Both the *Orthodox Jewish Bible* and the *New Messianic Bible* point out *'ĕlôhîym* in Hebrew means God. *The Orthodox Bible* puts a note in Psalm 8:5 of Genesis 1:27 which says God created man in His image. This is important to understand the high standing given to the first man and to realize this was God's desire. Evolution, humanism and even religion can lower man to a level God never intended. The correct order is God, man, angels.

Another aspect of man that is misunderstood is his spirit. Adam was a triune being with a spirit, a

---

[1] Genesis 1:26 says, "Let us make man in our image." God is The Father, Son and Holy Spirit.

soul and a body. But his spirit was to reign over his soul which is the mind, will and emotions. His spirit gave his body life, and this life was God's nature. God breathed life into Adam who was a pile of dirt in Genesis 2:7. Adam's spirit became the controlling force of his triune being. It is important for us study this.

1Thessalonians 5:23 lists man's triune nature as spirit, soul and body. Spirit is *pneuma* (NEWmah). *Thayer's Greek Lexicon* defines *pneuma* in this verse with its second meaning: the vital principle by which the body is animated. Soul is *psuchē* (sueHAY) which is related in usage to the Hebrew word *nephesh* (NAfish), the activity of the mind and will or the seat of emotion and passion.

Greek philosophers thought the soul was the highest part of man. Most educated professionals think the same today. God says no such thing, however.

In the Bible, *psuchē* is related to *psychikós* and *sarkikós*, and refers to the carnal, soulish or lower element of what makes man. This again is the mind, will and emotions. The man controlled by and acting out of this part of himself cannot receive or know the things of God because God is Spirit, and He speaks to man's spirit.

"But the natural [*psuchikos*] man receiveth not the things of the Spirit of God: for they are foolishness unto him: neither can he know them, because they are spiritually discerned." (1Co 2:14)

The body (*sōma*) is man's physical shell made up of his cells and systems. Man's five senses allow him to operate in and relate to the physical realm. When a man's spirit leaves his body, we say he has died. Actually, he has left his body, and the Bible compares this to laying aside a garment or tent. (2Peter 1:14)

God is Spirit and He gives life is a fact the Bible repeats from Old Testament to New. Here are two examples. "The Spirit of God hath made me, and the breath of the Almighty hath given me life." (Job 33:3) "... seeing he giveth to all life, and breath, and all things." (Acts 17:25) The idea that God gives life is not trivial because to be separated from God is to be separated from life.

When God created Adam, He shaped him with His hands. This reveals a completely different picture than how God created everything else. He spoke our world into existence, but man's body was formed as a husk in a unique way. Then God breathed into him.

Adam's spirit was to control his soul and to give life to his body. Another way to say this is that his spirit was to stay submissive to God, his soul submissive to his spirit and his body submissive to his soul. Soul and body therefore submit to the spirit.

Adam was a spirit man, and God gave Him the privilege of ruling over the earth. Adam's responsibility was to give joy to God through his fellowship with Him and to rule over the home God had created for him. In return, he would enjoy the fellowship and love of God.

In the Garden there were many beautiful trees, but two important ones were located at the center. One was called the tree of life and the other was named the tree of the knowledge of good and evil. The tree of life was God's tree, but the other tree became associated with someone else— Satan.

God established Adam in the Garden and informed him he could eat of any tree except one, and that was the tree of the knowledge of good and evil. If he ate from that tree, God told him he would die. The literal translation reads "for in the day that you eat of it, dying you shall die." (LITV) Dying you shall die was an exact picture of what would happen in the spirit first and then the body.

Later a serpent showed up and spoke to Eve, the first created woman. A speaking serpent didn't shock her or Adam so we can only wonder at the amazing creatures living in the Garden.

The serpent began by questioning her about God and His rules for them about the two trees. The serpent's timing is interesting. He just happened to be there? Not likely. It probably wasn't the first time Eve was standing near the tree.

Also interesting is that he didn't talk to Adam but it was clearly Adam whom he was after. The Jewish interpretation of the passage states that Adam was with Eve and heard the conversation. The Bible said the serpent was more cunning than any other creature. He understood Adam's authority better than Adam and may have already been planting thoughts in Adam's mind about the tree, hoping Adam would act on them.

The serpent told them they wouldn't die if they ate

from that tree. His announcement was a blatant lie and in direct opposition to God. He said if they ate from the tree they would know good and evil and be like God. His lie implied God was less than good because He was holding something back from them.

Jesus revealed this serpent to be Satan which means opponent, adversary or enemy. "And he laid hold on the dragon, that old serpent, which is the Devil, and Satan..." (Revelation 20:2)

Satan still uses the same tactics, making us doubt God and His goodness and then getting us to believe his lie. Jesus said about him, "He was a murderer from the beginning, and abode not in the truth, because there is no truth in him. When he speaketh a lie, he speaketh of his own: for he is a liar, and the father of it." (John 8:44)

Satan is a created being himself, an angel originally named Lucifer. He was beautiful and became full of pride. At some point, he led a rebellion against God with angels he had deceived. He wanted to take God's place but he lost. In the Garden, however, he set his sights on Adam and the world created for him.

Two things we should cover before we continue. The first is that Adam and Eve already knew good. What they didn't know was evil, and it seems God wanted to keep Adam from experiencing it, hence His warning. *Don't eat from that tree because you will die.*

Second, men, and obviously angels, have a free will. God considers having the ability to decide for yourself a perfect part of His creation. God didn't create robots He programmed. Man has a choice to follow God or not to follow God. And it is in the Garden we first learn that following God is good.

Eve was completely deceived by the serpent's words. Adam was not. He knew eating from the tree meant betraying God and forming an allegiance with this creature. He stood by listening, pondering and ignoring his responsibility to rule over the serpent and the Garden.

He began to separate from God. Adam saw with his eyes, thought with his mind and acted according to his emotions and will instead of being spirit led by God's words. He willfully disregarded God's warning and their bond of fellowship.

After Adam and Eve decided to use their free will and listen to their enemy and eat from the tree, they may have been relieved they didn't fall over dead. But something happened to the inside of them, in their spirit. It had separated from God who gave life.

Their minds began to darken (Ephesians 4:18) and they felt condemnation, guilt, fear and an atmosphere of doom over them. It was the first time they experienced any negative emotion. Their spirits were dying. It was a process, but neither Adam nor Eve expressed any sorrow over their betrayal, and neither asked for forgiveness.

They blamed God and each other. Since there was no remorse on their part, God could not offer mercy. It was an act done, and their enemy was the victor. Satan is also a spirit. (Eph 6:12) But his nature is death.

Why We Need to be Born Again

Adam and Eve were corrupted when they changed their spiritual overseers. Adam had only known God the Almighty. But he spiritually left God, binding himself spiritually to Satan and communing with him. Unlike God who protects and respects our free will, Satan forces everything he possibly can on us.

The separation from God was caused by disobedience to God's word. Romans 5:12 calls this disobedience sin and the separation death. "Adam sinned, and that sin brought death into the world." (CEV)

Next in Genesis we begin to read about murders, polygamy, jealousy, hatred, chaos and rebellion. Eventually there was disease and lameness. These were not part of the original creation. They were the result of Adam and Eve's spiritual death. This condition is what is called man's fallen nature because he fell from his high position in God and received a spirit of death which manifested in his physical body.

Their spiritual death was a permanent condition and became part of Adam's DNA he passed to his children. Adam as a man had the ability to impart life but that life was now inferior. Modern DNA research has shown "mammals" tend to be more like their father molecularly than their mother.[2] The Bible shows us for man this originates in the spiritual makeup of a person.

This is why Jesus could have no earthly father. God spoke to Mary, and she conceived the Word made flesh as John described Jesus in his opening chapter.

---

[2] Lamiat Sabin, "Why You're Almost Certainly More Like Your Father Than Your Mother," *Independent*, March 4, 2015.

When she agreed, "Let it be unto me according to your word," she became pregnant. (Luke 1:38) Jesus was fully God and became fully man, subject to all man's temptations through his mother not His father.

In Luke 4 we read about Jesus going into the wilderness to be tempted by Satan. At one point Satan offered Jesus all the power of the kingdoms on earth "for that is delivered unto me; and to whomsoever I will I give it." For once Satan wasn't lying or the temptation wouldn't have been real. Who delivered that power to him? Adam.

Adam discovered Satan is not only a deceitful murderer, he is a thief as well. What he wanted was Adam's authority over the earth so he could rule it. As soon as Adam sided with him, he took his authority.

Many people wonder why God made Satan. But if you read the Bible, you realize He didn't. Man created the Satan we know. Man gave him the authority he needed to take control of the earth. God created an angel who would serve to minister to man. The angel Satan who would rebel and lose was created subject to God and man with no authority. It was man, however, who supplied Satan with what he lacked.

It is because of Adam's sin man is now born into a position lower in rank than Satan and his demon spirits. Thanks to Adam's sin, mankind by default is spiritually linked to Satan instead of God. It is only through Jesus we break the mold, get restamped and made into the image of Jesus.

Adam and Eve learned physical death was part

of their new fallen condition too. Death is not natural to man. It was forced upon him by the fall. As time passed life expectancies began to diminish.

The spiritual affected the physical. This is the higher law God enacted when His Spirit gave life to Adam. This is the principle stated in Hebrews 11:3. "Through faith we understand that the worlds were framed by the word of God, so that things which are seen were not made of things which do appear."

The spirit of death gradually affected the earth. Animals became predators. The climate was no longer perfect. Disease and death fell upon plant and animal.

God did not want Adam and Eve to live in this death state forever so He made Adam leave the Garden where the tree of life stood. God did not want them to eat from it anymore. Revelations 22:1-3 speaks of this tree in heaven.

We don't see much of heaven on earth today because of this spiritual condition of man. Man's fallen nature is the result of sin which as we've discovered is disobeying or opposing God. Sin brings death as Adam was warned. Romans 6:23 says the wages of sin are death. You might think Satan would reward Adam for joining him in opposing God. He did. He paid him death. It was all he had.

Many believers like to think man is essentially good. That is not what the Bible says. Man was created good and perverted his goodness by his own choice. Man is now born into evil and sin, which produces death.

Before Jesus died on the cross and rose from the dead, Satan controlled death and kept people in bondage to the fear of it. (Hebrews 2:14) When the Bible says death reigned like a king (Romans 5:17), you must remember death is Satan's nature.

Many psychologists and educators believe if you create good environments, people will be good. But time has shown that not to be true. People can still lie, cheat and steal no matter what their upbringing or surroundings.

There must be something else at work in us to make us do what we do not want to do and what we know is wrong. This account in Genesis enlightens us to what the "something" is: a fallen spirit nature that has a personality of death.

Jesus told Nicodemus we will not see or understand how it happens but it is possible for man's spirit to be remade, born from above. John 3:8 says, "The wind bloweth where it listeth, and thou hearest the sound thereof, but canst not tell whence it cometh, and whither it goeth: so is every one that is born of the Spirit."

There are many who go through life questioning their purpose. They may be successful, using their free will to live moral lives, but are unfulfilled in the center of their being. The reason is they were not designed to live without God. They were created to fellowship with Him. There is nothing in their life that is a red arrow pointing to hideous sin, and yet they exist in man's fallen state. Their spirit is dead.

Many view being born again as sealing their destination after they die. They know if they accept Jesus' death on the cross for the forgiveness of their sins, they will live forever in heaven. It is true, and it is the reason people want to share the idea of becoming born again with others.

But being born again is not just a ticket to an eternal life as we will learn later. Everyone is eternal. Being born again makes you a part of God's family because it is His Spirit inside you. You become a citizen of the Kingdom of God at the moment you ask Jesus into your heart, and you are enabled to spend your eternal life in heaven– even better than the Garden of Eden.

Heaven is *shamayim* (shehMAyim) in Hebrew and *ouranos* (ooradhNAHS) in Greek and means probably what it means everywhere, a place in the sky where God lives, and it is happiness. You can say your vacation was heaven or even last night's steak, and everyone knows you mean it was perfect enjoyment.

But if you remain in a state of spiritual death, then you are separated from God by your choice and become a participant in your enemy's punishment. Hell was created for Satan. (Matt 25:41) Just like the meaning for heaven, everyone knows what hell is.

It is a lot worse than most people think, however. Jesus spoke more about hell than anyone else in the Bible. His message was clear. He doesn't want anyone to have to go there.

To demonstrate how terrible hell is, He said that if you have to gouge out your eye because it makes you sin, do it because it would be better to go through life with one eye than to have to go to hell. It will be where Satan lives.

Some Bible teachers claim that only people who believe in God have a free will. But how could that be? God is not unjust. If unbelievers did not have a free will how could they make any decisions for themselves? Even the decision to accept or reject Jesus? And, why try to tell others about being born again if they can't make a decision to accept Him?

No, all men have a free will, and they decide what they are doing with it. That is what the Bible states. "Choose this day whom you will serve," Joshua said. (Joshua 24:15) Hebrews 3 confirms our freedom to choose is still valid when it says, "Today if you hear His voice do not harden your hearts..." There are many other verses concerning our free will.

Why we need to be born again is because mankind suffered a spiritual death when Adam chose to disobey God and separate from His life giving nature. The result was sin, everything bad, and eventually physical death and all the things afflicting the body like disease.

The spiritual death affected the physical body and creation. Adam passed this quality on to his children, and it is why all mankind suffers in this state. It is how death entered God's creation and how Satan became the god of the earth.

A person who has not been born from above is walking around with a fallen spirit. It separates him from God, affects his physical and emotional state and ministers death to him even while he breathes. This was Nicodemus' condition, no matter how many rules he kept or how many chapters of God's word he had memorized.

If a man, like Nicodemus, wants to see the Kingdom of God, not just in eternity but here on earth, Jesus said he has to be born from above. God's Spirit of life living in a man causes him to be a different person. We will learn more about that in the next chapter.

Going Deeper

Define spirit, soul and body.

What is the highest part of man?

Explain the order of man's triune being as to how he should rule himself.

Describe what happened in the Garden.

Explain why it means more than Eve eating fruit.

What did it mean when God said "dying you shall die"?

What part of man needs to be reborn?

What is important for you to understand about Adam and Eve's experience?

How does understanding the truth about man's free will and fallen nature change the way you think about good and evil in the world?

How does it change what you think about other religious claims that don't represent Jesus as He is?

How does it change the way you think about God?

Chapter 4

The Result of Being Born Again

In the Garden Adam failed when he did not respect God's word or his responsibility. But there were men who came after Adam that did choose to honor God, and God used covenant agreements to bless them. One of those men was Abraham.

Because of God's promises to him, Abraham became the ancestor of the Israelites. Later, God gave the Israelites and their fledgling nation His laws for moral behavior and a religious system based on animal sacrifice for the forgiveness of sin.

The reason for the law was to teach God's standard of morality while showing them they could not keep this standard no matter how hard they tried. They needed help— a Savior who could release them from the cycle of sin and sacrifices.

God was faithful, gladly offering mercy and help until the Israelites broke their end of the covenant. They began worshipping other gods. These gods were Satan and his followers called demons. It was the same kind of betrayal as Adam's.

But the system of the law was not God's perfect solution. It was a method to teach man about himself. God's perfect answer to the problem of man's fallen nature was His new covenant. Hebrews 8:7-10 says:

> For if that first covenant had been faultless, then should no place have been sought for the second. For finding fault with them, he saith, Behold, the days come, saith the Lord, when I will make a new covenant with the house of Israel and with the house of Judah: Not according to the covenant that I made with their fathers in the day when I took them by the hand to lead them out of the land of Egypt; because they continued not in my covenant, and I regarded them not, saith the Lord. For this is the covenant that I will make with the house of Israel after those days, saith the Lord; I will put my laws into their mind, and write them in their hearts: and I will be to them a God, and they shall be to me a people.

Jesus' death and resurrection brought the new covenant into existence. God had made an agreement with anyone who wanted to enter into a relationship with Him. He had made the arrangements, accomplished the work of defeating sin and death with His own

The Result of Being Born Again

blood and power. All that was left was for someone to believe Him and accept His offer of becoming born anew, which would allow Him to put a new spirit in them and write His law on their heart.

In His conversation with Nicodemus, Jesus alluded to His crucifixion when He said, "And as Moses lifted up the serpent in the wilderness, even so must the Son of man be lifted up: That whosoever believeth in him should not perish, but have eternal life." (John 3: 14-15)

Nicodemus had to know the story of the bronze snake well. (Numbers 21) During one of their episodes of grumbling against God and separating from Him, the freed Israelite slaves had been overrun with poisonous snakes in their camps. After many people had died from snake bites, a delegation came to Moses and asked him to pray to God for help.

God told Moses to make a bronze snake and fasten it to a pole. Whenever anyone was bitten by a snake, all they had to do was look up at the bronze snake on the pole and they would not die.

Nicodemus must have been shocked as the cry to crucify Jesus met his ears later in Jerusalem. The image of the bronze snake in the story must have seared his mind's eye as he witnessed Jesus lifted up on the cross. Surely he remembered Jesus' words that fateful night as he looked up at the blood covered young "rabbi".

You may wonder why God didn't place this born again part earlier in history. But when you understand the Bible as a whole, you realize God has appointed times for His plans to unfold. This included when He would send Jesus to die on the cross.

He had this plan in place from the beginning. While God did not make Adam decide to disobey, He is all knowing. Therefore He knew the choice Adam would make. We can see God's timeline for Jesus coming to the earth in a prophecy given to Daniel. It says:

> Know, then, and understand that from the going out of a word to restore and to rebuild Jerusalem, to Messiah the Prince, shall be seven weeks and sixty two weeks. The street shall be built again, and the wall, even in times of affliction. And after sixty two weeks, Messiah shall be cut off, but not for Himself. (Daniel 9:25-26 LITV)

The decree to rebuild the Temple and Jerusalem came in 455BC through King Artaxerxes. (Nehemiah 2) Doing the math and understanding that Jews used a lunar calendar which makes a year 360 days, scholars figured out Jesus' Triumphant Entry into Jerusalem was around 32AD. The book of Daniel is one of the books that can be documented historically. This makes the prophecy that much more remarkable in that it was recorded hundreds of years before Jesus was born.

But by the time of Jesus' birth, Simeon was the only man in Jerusalem recorded as looking for the Messiah. (Luke 2:25) Apparently he knew the prophecies, per-

The Result of Being Born Again

haps including this one. The wise men from the east could have been familiar with Daniel's prophecy too, since Daniel had lived in Babylon and was a high ranking official. Daniel even prophesied the fall of Babylon which probably brought him some attention don't you think?

Jesus expressed His disappointment that none of the Jewish religious hierarchy understood or recognized the "time of their visitation" which Daniel and the other prophets foretold. (Luke 19:41-44) When Jesus informed his disciples the Temple would be destroyed they were surprised. But that too was prophesied by Daniel, right after the bit about the Messiah.

God's first announcement of a plan to send a Deliverer was heard in the Garden of Eden. Speaking to the serpent God said, "And I will put enmity between thee and the woman, and between thy seed and her seed; it shall bruise thy head, and thou shalt bruise his heel." (Genesis 3:15) *It* in this verse is the Hebrew *hû'* which can also mean he.

Galatians 3:16 identified this seed as Jesus who descended from Abraham. "Now to Abraham and his seed were the promises made. He saith not, And to seeds, as of many; but as of one, And to thy seed, which is Christ."

God's covenant agreement with Abraham was not based upon the law. The law came much later. Genesis 15:6 says Abraham believed what God told him and it was credited to him as righteousness. This is taught again in Romans 4 where it says protection and provision in Jesus and in this new covenant comes by grace through faith. This was the same process Abraham used. (Romans 4 and 5 are excellent chapters to read to learn about righteousness by faith and the purpose of the law.)

1Corinthians 15:45 says Jesus became like a second Adam. "And so it is written, The first man Adam was made a living soul; the last Adam was made a quickening spirit." Notice that it says Adam was made, *ginomai* to cause to be; to become, a living soul, *psuchē,* the lower element of man. The focus is the fallen state.

Quickening is the word *zōopoieō* (zoh ah pah AY oh). It means to make alive or to restore to life. The verse is saying Jesus/God is imparting life by His Spirit. The purpose is to restore man's position as if Adam never sinned.

Romans 5:19 explains, "For as by one man's disobedience many were made sinners, so by the obedience of one shall many be made righteous." The man who brought disobedience was Adam. The one who brought righteousness was Jesus.

But Jesus came to earth about four thousand years after Adam. In the meantime, while Old Testament believers were waiting for their Deliverer, God used covenants to protect those who trusted in Him and used the system of law and sacrifice to cover their sin.

So to review, God made this covenant process known to Abraham, and Abraham took Him up on it by believing and trusting Him. God extended Abraham's covenant to his descendants, the Israelites.

The Result of Being Born Again

After the Israelites left Egypt, God gave them a code of moral conduct and standards. But the law only proved that man was not capable of being moral or righteous on his own. It only brought attention to his spiritual condition and his failure to behave according to the Ten Commandments.

The law also revealed a cycle of sin and death and showed a relationship between them. Sin brought death but sacrifice brought forgiveness. Romans 6:23 says the wages of sin are death. But Jesus came to set us free through a spiritual rebirth.

This is why Jesus in his conversation with Nicodemus focused on the Spirit not the law. Nicodemus was an expert in the law and the required sacrifices. But Jesus was revealing another higher, better covenant for those who wanted it. This confused Nicodemus.

He understood that in the past the Holy Spirit of God would come upon a prophet, king or person to accomplish something they could not do without help. Like Samson's amazing feats of strength or Elijah's fantastic miracles. But Jesus was talking of God's Spirit coming *into* a man to dwell there.

2Corinthians 5:17 says this process creates a new species of man that has never lived before. "Therefore if any man be in Christ, he is a new creature: old things are passed away; behold, all things are become new." It is Jesus' death and resurrection that brought about this new dimension for believers.

As a new creation we change addresses in the spiritual realm. We move out of the kingdom of darkness, which is Satan's domain, and into the kingdom of light. Since God is light and there is no darkness in Him and Jesus is the light of the world, this kingdom of light belongs to God.

Colossians 1:12-14 says "giving thanks to the Father, who made us fit to be partakers of the inheritance of the saints in light; who delivered us out of the power of darkness, and translated us into the kingdom of the Son of his love; in whom we have our redemption through his blood, the forgiveness of our sins." (WEB)

Redemption means being bought back. Jesus bought us with His blood when He suffered on the cross at His crucifixion. Some call it the great exchange. He took all the sin and its curse upon Himself and gave us the opportunity to receive His holiness. Notice that it is an opportunity, however.

You might wonder what we were redeemed from. We were redeemed from the curse of the law written in Deuteronomy 28:15-68 and the law of sin and death enacted by Adam's sin. "Christ hath redeemed us from the curse of the law, being made a curse for us." (Galatians 3:13) Romans 8:1-2 says, "There is therefore now no condemnation to them which are in Christ Jesus, who walk not after the flesh, but after the Spirit. For the law of the Spirit of life in Christ Jesus hath made me free from the law of sin and death."

When God gave the Ten Commandments and His system of animal sacrifice for forgiving the Israelites' sins, He told them if they did what He outlined for them to do they could expect to be blessed because that is how His kingdom works. Obedience, love and relationship allow God to work on your behalf and give Him the ability to bless you with all things for life. God is good but He doesn't force Himself on you. You must make the decision to choose Him.

If the Israelites chose not to obey, then they separated from God and were under Satan's dominion and the opposite of everything good because he is the opposite of everything that is God. The opposite of a blessing is a curse, and the curses listed in Deuteronomy 28 are what Jesus took upon Himself on the cross— all those and the sin of the world.

The system of blessings for those who follow Jesus is still in operation. So are the curses for those who are outside of God's kingdom. Jesus' blood is like the sacrificial lamb of Passover. It wipes away sin and makes you acceptable to God. The effects of death pass over those cleansed by Jesus' blood.

Some Christians say Jesus' blood covers their sin. But it doesn't cover it; Jesus' blood completely erases sin so that God doesn't even remember it anymore. (Hebrews 8:12) If He doesn't remember it, neither should you. Satan is *diabolos,* the accuser, and he works to keep a born again person fixated on their past fallen state to convince them they are still fallen and worthless. That way they will never live in the victory and authority Jesus won for them.

From the very beginning, God made a way for all who are separated from Him in our fallen sin state to come into a relationship with Him just because He wanted to do this for us. It is done through His grace and mercy, and He did it because He loves everyone and doesn't want anyone to die, so says 2Peter 3:9. Jesus died when no one understood what He was doing.

This condition of being spiritually born from above, or born again, is what is called salvation. Ephesians 2:1-5 explains this:

> You were made alive when you were dead through trespasses and sins, in which you once walked according to the course of this world, according to the prince of the powers of the air, of the spirit who now works in the sons of disobedience; among whom we also all once lived in the lust of our flesh, doing the desires of the flesh and of the mind, and were by nature children of wrath, even as the rest. But God, being rich in mercy, for his great love with which he loved us, even when we were dead through our trespasses, made us alive together with Christ (by grace have you been saved).

You were made alive. Jesus lives in you the moment you are born again. (Ephesians 3:17) But Jesus didn't just save us for heaven. His death and resurrection won back man's position to rule the earth. "... having stripped the rulers and the authorities, He made a show of them in public, triumphing over them in it." (Colossians 2:15 LITV)

When you are born again you are a new creature indeed. Jesus as the second Adam restored man's position of dominance over Satan. Jesus said in Matthew 28:18-20 that all authority had been given to Him.

In Luke 10:19 He said, "Behold, I give unto you power to tread on serpents and scorpions, and over all the power of the enemy: and nothing shall by any means hurt you." If we didn't have authority over Satan and his demons, we would not have been told that if we resist him he will flee. (James 4:7 and 1Peter 5:9) Jesus is in us after all. "... greater is he that is in you, than he that is in the world." (1John 4:4)

The result of being born again is salvation, living life rescued from a cycle of sin, defeat, failure and guilt. It is to experience victory over sin and possess a future, on earth and in heaven. It is to be made brand new from the inside out as the Spirit of life dwells inside your heart. Remember, Jesus is alive in you. This is important for you to understand.

The result of being born again is to be repositioned in accordance with your original design and enabled to fulfill your purpose. It means experiencing the love and mercy of your Creator. His desire for you may be seen in His covenants that promise to bless, protect and provide.

You do have responsibilities because of your new birth. You are expected to take your position against Satan's work in the world and in your life to defeat him in Jesus' name.

Also, it is your spirit that has been reborn, but it is your job to see that your mind is renewed. Most Christians start their believing life by reading the Bible but fall into the habit of relying on what others think the Bible is saying. Bible reading is not a priority in their life, and devotions are the quick kind, five, ten, or fifteen minutes and done. Usually these types of devotions feature one verse.

You are going to need a better foundation than that to know Jesus and the depth of His truths for you. In Matthew 13 there are four types of believers in the Parable of the Sower. Three out of the four gave a place to their enemy because they did not value or understand the word given to them. You can make it to heaven if you are one of the three, earlier perhaps than you wanted. But, you can do better and be that one kind of believer with good soil.

To do this, your spirit must rule your soul. Romans 12:2 says, "And be not conformed to this world: but be ye transformed by the renewing of your mind, that ye may prove what is that good, and acceptable, and perfect, will of God."

The way to renew your mind is to read and think about God's words to you which is the Bible. Deeply thinking, pondering, is the way to meditate on God's word. Submit to the Spirit of God inside you because He is your Teacher. (John 14:26) He bears witness with our spirit is the principle (Romans 8:16) and conveys the truth of the Word to our mind.

Some Bible teachers say we can never know the

The Result of Being Born Again

things of God, quoting 1Corinthians 2:9. But the verse is contrasting the non-born again person with one who is a new creation because in the same passage it says these things were revealed to the Christian through the Holy Spirit. It concludes in verse sixteen, saying to the Christian, "But you have the mind of Christ."

How did you get the mind of Christ? "Now we have received, not the spirit of the world, but the spirit which is of God; that we might know the things that are freely given to us of God." (1Corinthians 2:12)

Then you must put into practice what you learn. Proving involves doing. If you just read but never do, you will not live a successful Christian life. If you resist Satan's attacks and control your thoughts to agree with God, you will experience life and peace. (Romans 8 and Isaiah 26:3)

Remember staying in the place where God can bless you involves being obedient to His word. Obedience to God's methods is required to be blessed and have peace and confidence before God and to fellowship with Him freely. But obedience isn't what saves you; it is how you show that you love God and honor His word. (John 14:15) Jesus has granted you salvation. It is a gift. You can never earn it.

By now you probably realize being born again is not just a mental activity. It is not just something you pray in hopes that after you die it promises a good future. Being born again changes you on a level you are not even aware you own. But if you don't know what it means, you will never take advantage of all it does and offers. You truly will be just waiting for heaven and trying to survive this world and Satan's attacks by your wits.

In the next chapter we will take a look at the benefits of being born again.

Going Deeper

What was the purpose of the laws in the Old Testament?

Why is Abraham important to Christians?

Why did Jesus focus on the Spirit not the Law in His conversation with Nicodemus?

Explain why Jesus is called the second Adam.

Why is a Christian called a new creation?

Why does Satan want you focused on your sin?

What is the result of being born again?

What are your responsibilities as a born again Christian? Rewrite your answer as a prayer.

Chapter 5

Benefits of Being Born Again

In the last chapter we learned being born again results in your salvation and a move to the Kingdom of Light. Salvation includes more than a guarantee of heaven. It restores your place of authority and dominion on the earth as if Adam never sinned.

So, what is salvation? Eph 2:8 says, "For by grace are ye saved through faith; and that not of yourselves: it is the gift of God." Salvation is called a gift many times in the Bible. We receive it by grace through faith. One way to look at it is grace is God's part and faith is our part.

The biblical defintion of faith is *pistis*, putting your trust, belief, assurance or confidence in something. Grace is *charis*, (KAREiss) liberality, pleasure, favor, benefit and joy. Joy is *chara* and is derived from *charis*. Joy comes out of grace is the idea.

This favor and pleasure is God's motivation for salvation. Out of His pleasure, goodwill and joy God provided a way of salvation, and all we need to do is trust in Him and take His gift.

In Ephesians 2:8, saved is translated from the Greek word *sōzo* (SO-dzoe). According to *Thayer's Greek Lexicon*, *sōzo* means to save, to keep safe and sound, to rescue from danger or destruction, to make well, to heal, restore to health. *Strong's* defines it as to save, keep safe and sound, to rescue from danger or destruction; to save a suffering one (from perishing), i.e. one suffering from disease, to make well, heal, restore to health.

Sōzo is spoken of in some verses as an earthly possession and in others as a future possession because it is both. It is a blessing begun on earth and perfected when Jesus returns for those who are His. (1Thessalonians 4:16-17 and 1Corinthians 15:52)

Jesus told Nicodemus being born from above was the only way to see the kingdom, and He meant on earth or in heaven. According to Jesus, being born again makes you a new creation. He said whoever trusts in Him will be free because His life in you breaks any yokes put upon you to enslave you to addictions, emotions, disease, poverty, etc. (Luke 4:18-19)

It lifts your burdens, heals and enables you to understand the things of God because you have entered in as Jesus taught in Luke 8:11-18. But this freedom is available to you only as you understand it is your responsibility to receive it.

It is vital that you focus on the biblical definition of saved and not what tradition teaches. Tradition teaches that these benefits are only spiritual and reserved for when we get to heaven. That is not how the word *sōzo* is used in the Bible. It was used to refer to present situations too.

For example, the disciples used the word in Matthew 8:25 when they were in danger of drowning. The woman with the issue of blood used it when she wanted healing. Peter used it when he began to sink while walking on water. Jairus used it when he wanted his daughter healed.

Jesus used it pertaining to healing many times. He used the word both for healing and salvation as in Mark 3:4 and the Parable of the Sower in Luke 8:12. And it continued to be used for both the present and future in the book of Acts.

Salvation is a blessing that begins on earth. It is a new privilege. You begin walking in the eternal, everlasting life the minute you are born again. It is a spiritual benefit package to restore you to life. For example, Jesus never preached on how to be healed. He preached the kingdom and the Good News.

When He said the kingdom was at hand, Jesus was declaring the time of His reign upon the earth was beginning. He was establishing His kingdom and His dominion on earth through His followers. "The kingdom is within you," He said. (Luke 17:20-21)

Jesus announced in a Nazareth synagogue what this kingdom reign included:

> And there was delivered unto him the book of the prophet Esaias. And when he had opened the book, he found the

place where it was written, "The Spirit of the Lord is upon me, because he hath anointed me to preach the gospel to the poor; he hath sent me to heal the brokenhearted, to preach deliverance to the captives, and recovering of sight to the blind, to set at liberty them that are bruised, To preach the acceptable year of the Lord." And he closed the book, and he gave it again to the minister, and sat down. And the eyes of all them that were in the synagogue were fastened on him. And he began to say unto them, "This day is this scripture fulfilled in your ears."(Luke 4:17-21)

Jesus began distinguishing His work from Satan's by exposing demons and healing every kind of malady and disease. He began setting things right and authorizing His disciples to do the same. He introduced us to the kingdom through His ministry and enabled it through His death and resurrection to be a living entity for anyone who trusted in Him.

When Jesus said, "It is finished," He was speaking of His work and the system of animal sacrifices. Our forgiveness is a finished work. Our healing is a finished work. A born again believer is not waiting to be forgiven, and they are not waiting to be healed. Both are yours now through the blood of Jesus.

God's will for you on earth is the same as His will

for you in heaven. Jesus said we are to pray that God's will in heaven be done upon the earth. "After this manner therefore pray ye: Our Father which art in heaven, Hallowed be thy name. Thy kingdom come. Thy will be done in earth, as it is in heaven." (Matthew 6:9-10)

What is happening in heaven? Illness? Disease? Lack? You would think so by what many teach about God's will concerning healing. They confuse God's work with what is Satan's.

There is no integrity in a message that says God uses pain and illness to teach His people spiritual lessons when as soon as we are afflicted we seek a doctor to rid ourselves of "God's will." If the work of Satan in our life has made us realize something is wrong, that is our doing because somehow we are separated from God in our actions or thinking or unaware of our enemy. We can't blame God for our ignorance.

But He stands by waiting to help. Delays happen when we think God gave us our problems. We are left in a state of limbo trying to figure out what we need to learn. Here is what we need to learn: God doesn't give us sickness. Satan does.

If pain and suffering turned people to God, the entire world should be born again. The point of Jesus' suffering the curse was so we wouldn't have to. Our "suffering" involves people not liking Christians and disciplining ourselves not to be led by our soulish selves. It is standing against Satan's attacks. We do not have to suffer the things included in the curse. Jesus has made us free, indeed!

Born Again: Not Just For Heaven

Missionary Tim Born in one Sunday's message hoped to dispel the confusion when he repeated over and over, "God is good; the devil is bad." James 1:17 says it this way, "Every good gift and every perfect gift is from above, and cometh down from the Father of lights, with whom is no variableness, neither shadow of turning." To enjoy our benefits as born again believers we need to understand God is good.

Jesus' finished work guarantees if you mess up and sin, you repent and are immediately restored to peace. If you are assaulted with sickness, it is possible to receive healing. If you are in danger, it is possible to receive deliverance. Jesus said nothing will be impossible to you. But He warned it was according to what you believe. "If thou canst believe, all things are possible to him that believeth." (Mark 9:23)

Sōtēria (sotayRHEEah) is another word used for salvation. It means to save, deliver, rescue, health and salvation. It is used for health in Acts 27:34. Acts was written by a born again physician named Luke. He wrote in a sophisticated style of Greek, and was the only Gentile author of one of the Gospels.

When he told the account of how Peter explained salvation to the Jewish priests in Acts 4:9-12, he used both *sōzo* and *sōtēria* and another word *hugiēs* (whogheeACE) which means to be made well bodily, sound or restored. Luke knew the language well, and he understood what word to use for healing because he was a doctor.

In this passage, the priests had asked Peter about a

Benefits of Being Born Again

lame man he had healed. Let's take a look at Peter's reply and how Luke recorded the meaning of the event by the words he chose.

> If we are examined today on a good work for an infirm man, by what this one has been healed,[*sōzo*] be it known to you all, and to all the people of Israel, that by the name of Jesus Christ of Nazareth, whom you crucified, whom God raised from the dead, in this name does this man stand before you whole. [*hugiēs*] This is the Stone which you builders have counted worthless, and He has become the Head of the Corner. And there is salvation [*sōtēria*], in no other One; for there is no other name under Heaven given among men by which we must be saved. [*sōzo*]
> Acts 4:9-12(LITV)

Pentecostal and Charismatic Christians believe healing is part of their salvation based on this account in Acts and many other verses. For example two such verses are Psalm 103 and Mark 2. Psalm 103:2-4 says:

> Bless the LORD, O my soul, and forget not all his benefits: Who forgiveth all thine iniquities; who healeth all thy diseases; Who redeemeth thy life from

destruction; who crowneth thee with lovingkindness and tender mercies...

Let's take a look at some word meanings in this Psalm and make sure they mean what we think they mean. Benefits is *gemûl* (ghemMOOL) and means that which is given, a reward or service. Iniquities is *'âvôn* (ahVone). It means perversity or fault, a sin. Heal is *râphâh* (ruhFAH) meaning to repair, heal, cure, to make whole. It is the word for physician. Redeem is *gâ'al* (GahAl) and it means to buy back or ransom.

It is the same meaning as *apolutrōsis* (uhpolOOtrosis) in Ephesians 1:7 which states that we have redemption through Jesus' blood and forgiveness. Life is *chay* (HIGH) meaning alive. It is the same word used in Genesis 1 and in 2:7 where it says man became a living creature, *chay nephesh*.

We see then there is the idea that God's benefits or rewards include the forgiveness of sin and bodily healing, the act of being made whole. Jesus also connected these ideas when he healed the paralytic in Mark 2. Some of the religious people present were offended that Jesus told the man his sins had been forgiven.

But Jesus asked them, "Which is easier? To say to the paralytic, your sins are forgiven, or to say, rise up; take your bed and walk?" This account implies Jesus considered them the same.

If death entered into the world through sin as we have learned, and diseases were in the curse, and if we are free from the law of sin and death, then truly by

Jesus' stripes we were healed when we were forgiven. Isaiah prophesied those very words, by His stripes we are healed, in Isaiah 53:4. The Holy Spirit, speaking through Matthew, points to the verse concerning Jesus healing all who came to Him. (Matthew 8:16-17)

But Peter puts the idea in the past tense. "... by whose stripes ye were healed." (1Peter 2:24) Why? Because Peter was writing after Jesus rose from the dead. Jesus' blood bought us both forgiveness and healing because they are connected.

You might ask why people aren't healed of their diseases today if they are saved. The answer is most people think God is able to heal, but aren't sure if He wants to. They don't believe it is already done for them because they separate forgiveness and healing. They think they have to ask and ask and ask and beg God, go without food and get hundreds of people to barrage heaven with a prayer chain. Then maybe, *if* God wants to heal you, He will. Most believe He uses sickness.

But the reality is you receive healing the same way you get saved. You believe what God said, you trust in Him to receive it and confess it with your mouth. You don't surrender your trust and confession for any circumstance because it is done. If you don't believe healing is already yours, you probably won't experience it. Many Christians believe it, and have testimonies to prove it.

Healing is part of our salvation package, mental and physical. Deliverance or help through dangers is another benefit. Salvation grafts us into the covenant

God gave Abraham. (Romans 11:11-31) Whatever benefits Abraham enjoyed so can we. The blessings in Deuteronomy 28 are God's perfect will and desire for you.

Deuteronomy 7:15 says, "And the LORD will take away from thee all sickness." Study the life of Jesus and you will see the Father's heart toward His people–perfect compassion and a willingness to help them.

About those covenants—

To be clear, when God made His covenant agreement with the Israelites, He didn't abolish the one He had made with Abraham. He couldn't. He fulfilled His promises and upheld them as long as the Israelites kept their part of the agreement.

But the covenants were never cancelled after God made a new one. God waited for someone to keep them so He could bless them. "Know therefore that the LORD thy God, he is God, the faithful God, which keepeth covenant and mercy with them that love him and keep his commandments to a thousand generations." (Deuteronomy 7:9)

In Deuteronomy 7, God explains that He will keep His covenant and mercy to those that love Him. *Checed* (khehsed) is the word we translate as mercy, but it also means kindness, lovingkindness, goodness and favor. According to Professor Elinoar Bareket of Achva Academic College, *chesed* in the Bible refers most of the time to the way a stronger party acts toward the other in a covenant relationship, God towards His people.[1]

[1] Elinoar Bareket. "Chesed: A Reciprocal Covenant," *The Torah.com*, 2017. https://www.thetorah.com/article/chesed-a-reciprocal-covenant

When you see the words mercy, lovingkindness, goodness, kindness and favor in the Old Testament, you are seeing a reference to God's covenant. *Chesed* is a covenant word. It can be formed between people like the covenant of *chesed* between Jonathan and David. But mostly it concerns God's covenant with those who love Him. God's covenant of *chesed* includes protection and deliverance from enemies.

This brings us to a question. If God gave them covenants to bless them, why were there so many sick, lame Israelites during the time of Jesus? The reasons are varied but are applicable to us today. First many weren't keeping the laws of the covenant. The reason Israel no longer ruled their own country was because they had walked away from their covenants and served idols instead. They separated from God.

For those that were serving God, their teachers, like Nicodemus, had little understanding of how Satan worked and thought God gave them sickness as a punishment or to teach them something. They also had no authority over Satan and his work.

In Luke 5:12 we are introduced to a man suffering with leprosy, one of the most dreaded diseases of the time. He was a Jew, of Abraham's family and heir to the covenants and yet he asked, "Lord if you are willing, you can make me clean." Why didn't he know what God's will was? Because of the same misunderstandings about God that still exist. Mainly, that God gave or allowed the sickness to punish or teach the person afflicted; it was not an attack from the enemy.

Satan does attack. He seeks out a victim to tempt with thoughts that will separate them from God's word and focus them on the body or soul. An unwary Christian is the best target, but a healthy one is a threat. The battle will come to you at some point. How you handle it depends on what you know about God.

The covenants are not void today. Ephesians 2:12-13 says, "That at that time ye were without Christ, being aliens from the commonwealth of Israel, and strangers from the covenants of promise, having no hope, and without God in the world: But now in Christ Jesus ye who sometimes were far off are made nigh by the blood of Christ."

When a person becomes born again they are one in Christ, in fellowship with God and other believers and an heir to those promises. All the laws pertaining to sacrifices and washing were abolished, however.

Jesus did not do away with the Old Testament agreement but improved it as Hebrews 8 tells us. His death and resurrection ended the need for animal sacrifices. His blood was enough to cleanse all sins for all generations. All that is needed to gain access to God's promises of blessing through faith is for you to receive the gift of salvation Jesus gave you. He has fully met all conditions for our opportunity to enjoy God's blessings.

Another upgrade to Old Testament covenants is you have authority against Satan because Jesus gave it back to you. Satan is defeated as long as you enforce your authority and give him no place in your life. Also, you are now seated in heavenly places according to

Ephesians 2:6. Ephesians is a book to read to understand your identity as a born again member of God's family. So is the book of Romans and Galatians 3.

A born again believer is a son of God, a member of God's family and a joint heir with Jesus. "But as many as received him, to them gave he power to become the sons of God, even to them that believe on his name." (John 1:12) Other verses and translations say children of God.

The point is, you are family, and if family then an heir. Romans 8:16-17 says, "The Spirit itself beareth witness with our spirit, that we are the children of God: And if children, then heirs; heirs of God, and joint-heirs with Christ."

It is in God's family, and as a citizen of God's kingdom, true equality is realized. Galatians 3:28 states, "There is neither Jew nor Greek, there is neither bond nor free, there is neither male nor female: for ye are all one in Christ Jesus." Your identity is in Jesus the moment you are born again.

There are no separating elements like status or race inside God's kingdom because you are a spirit. These classifications are according to your body and soul, the lowest element of man and were not part of creation. They are from Satan's divisive nature and rooted in his culture of the world.

Holy Spirit baptism is another privilege of being born again. In Acts 2 Jesus' followers "were all filled with the Holy Ghost, and began to speak with other tongues, as the Spirit gave them utterance." The Holy

Spirit gave them power to witness and minister in Jesus' name. Jesus said when "he Spirit of truth, is come, he will guide you into all truth." (John 16:13)

The baptism of the Holy Spirit is yours for the asking when you are born again. He is called the Comforter and Advocate or Helper. Satan may be your adversary but he has been defeated, and you have an Advocate.

The reality is the God of the universe has taken up residence inside your heart, the center of your very being, upon your invitation. It is why 1John 4:17 can state "that as He is, we are also in this world." God's love has restored our dignity in Him.

It is important to meditate on these verses because most believers experience a small fraction of the benefits Jesus won for them. 1Timothy 4:15 says, "Meditate upon these things; give thyself wholly to them; that thy profiting may appear to all."

As a born again member of God's own family and a citizen of His kingdom, you have prayer privileges. You can boldly approach God with your requests, and if they line up with what He has freely given you in His word and according to His moral standards, He has promised to answer you. What you cannot do, is impose your will over another's. If your neighbor demands to remain an atheist, ill, etc., he may use his free will to do so.

Jesus said if you remain in Him and His words remain in you, you can ask whatever you desire and it will be done. Remain is *menō* (MEHNoh), to stay, to continue, to dwell. This implies a familiarity and in-

Benefits of Being Born Again

timacy in a relationship to God and His word. It also implies a firm faith, not doubting His promises which is another lesson.

To sum up, your born again benefit package provides a life of abundant provision and help on earth, health, intimacy with the Father, authority over Satan, the privilege of forgiveness for your sins and guaranteed victory over death because you will live your eternal life with Him.

And about heaven—

Born again believers do go to heaven when they die. The Bible compares dying for the believer to falling asleep. We fall asleep and wake up somewhere else. As soon as we leave our body, we are with Jesus. There is no pain associated with death. But we are coming back to the earth to rule it (Revelation 20-21), and eternity looks busy.

Perhaps now you can understand why Jesus said in John 10:10 that He brings abundant life. "The thief cometh not, but for to steal, and to kill, and to destroy: I am come that they might have life, and that they might have it more abundantly." Abundantly is *perissos* (paydrheeSAHS), meaning over and above, superior in quality, more excellent.

This may be different from what you've learned about being born again. But this is what the Bible says about becoming a member of God's kingdom. "According as his divine power hath given unto us all things that pertain unto life and godliness, through the knowledge of him that hath called us to glory and virtue." (2Peter 1:3)

Nicodemus may have been shocked to think the covenant blessings and Jesus the Messiah would also be offered to non Jews. But he surely didn't miss the words God so loved the world...

His leaders and fellow priests, the same who crucified Jesus, pursued early Christians, jailing and killing them. But what about their promises, you ask? Jesus laid down His life. He came to the earth to die on the cross for us. But He said in John 15 that if the world hated Him, it is going to hate you. Jesus was mocked and scorned. You will be too.

You will be living under a different set of rules established by a different government, God's kingdom. It doesn't run according to the world's wisdom. Its wisdom created the world and exists on a higher level. Operating in it will seem like foolishness to people who do not understand it and live through the reasoning in their minds influenced by a spirit of death. But they have never walked on water, healed the sick and calmed storms with a word.

In addition, becoming born again makes you dangerous to your enemy. He will circle you looking for a weak spot to get into your thoughts and create a foothold, a place from which he can work. He will bombard you with circumstances trying to get you to let go of your confidence in God. He uses fear like God uses faith.

His goal is to make you ineffective as a believer. Peter tells you to be alert, submit to God and resist Satan. (1Peter 5:8-9) Peter learned how to do this and still died for his commitment to Jesus later in his life. The important thing is he knew when it was his time to die. He didn't volunteer early.

The key is staying sensitive to God's voice and knowing your authority. Not every Christian is called to be a martyr. We are called to be different, and sometimes different attracts insult, hardship and hatred. Even so, while some may be martyred, some are delivered.

We are all called to be more than conquerors so don't lie down before the enemy. Humble yourself before God. There is a difference. We need to expect God's protection and rescue. Like Esther. Like Daniel. Like Shadrach, Meshach, and Abednego. Born again Christians need to understand their covenant of *chesed* like these giants of the faith. They need to fully realize who they are in Jesus.

Remember, Peter was delivered a few times too. He walked out of prison and around Jerusalem while others were being dragged out of their homes. Paul had a list of victorious rescues. Jesus walked invisible through the crowd that wanted to throw Him off a cliff. The lesson is God causes us to always triumph over the enemy no matter what the circumstances.

But only if you are born again.

Going Deeper

What is God's motivation to provide salvation?

Define salvation.

List the benefits of being born again.

Does this definition of salvation and list of benefits differ from what you've been taught? Explain.

Choose three scripture references from this chapter to study and think about. Ask God to speak to you through them. Write down what you learn.

Chapter 6

The Purpose of Being Born Again

Many Christians misunderstand the concept of being born again. They would probably say that being born again is the way to get your sin forgiven and go to heaven when you die. They stop at the word perish in John 3:16. "For God so loved the world, that he gave his only begotten Son, that whosoever believeth in him should not perish, but have everlasting life."

For the average Christian the goal is the forgiveness of sin and going to heaven. But if you read the entire verse the purpose is to have everlasting life. Have is in the present tense. The moment you believe in Jesus you have it.

Of course, removing sin is necessary because it is in the way. Sin produces death which is the separation from God and keeps us in a state of ignorance and rejection of all that is God.

Jesus told Nicodemus that whoever believed in the Son would not die but have everlasting life. But everlasting life is not just living forever. Everyone will live forever. (Matt 25:46) So what is it?

Jesus defined everlasting life in His prayer during the Last Supper. Speaking of Himself Jesus said, "You gave to Him authority over all flesh, so that to all which You gave to Him, He may give to them everlasting life. And this is everlasting life, that they may know You, the only true God, and Jesus Christ, whom You have sent." John 17:2-3 (LITV)

Know in this verse is *ginōskō* (ghenOHskoh). It means to have knowledge of and is the same word used to describe the intimacy between a man and wife. This is the depth of the relationship God is offering to one who is born again. The most important aspect of being born again is related to Adam's original purpose, to fellowship with God.

Jesus told His followers they would know, *ginōskō*, that He was living in them. "...because I live, ye shall live also. At that day ye shall know that I am in my Father, and ye in me, and I in you." (John 14:19-20) Several verses tell us Jesus comes into our hearts when we are born again. 2Corinthians 13:5 and Romans 8:10, for example. This provides us with intimacy and knowledge of Him. It is how we may know the mind of Christ and have the Spirit of revelation.

Jesus revealed how important having this deep intimate relationship is when He said there could be those who healed in His name or cast out demons but never knew (*ginōskō*) Him. This type of knowing means loving and having an atmosphere of submission and cooperation. He will reject those not willing to enter into this intimate relationship.

> Many will say to me in that day, Lord, Lord, have we not prophesied in thy name? and in thy name have cast out devils? and in thy name done many wonderful works? And then will I profess unto them, I never knew you: depart from me, ye that work iniquity.
> (Matthew 7:22-23)

This passage also reveals how important obedience to the word is. Many people see those who do miraculous signs and healings as being obvious followers of God and hold them up as esteemed believers. God, however, honors the obedient and those in an intimate relationship with Him.

Signs and wonders are expected to follow believers, but not at the expense of the relationship or respecting and obeying the word. A true believer will give first place to God's word and practice it.

To take advantage of all that is yours as a born again believer, you have to understand what you have and mix it with trust in God. If all you know is the forgiveness of sins and life in heaven, you probably won't receive all that is due you. 2Peter 1:2-4 tells us all of it comes through our knowledge, *epignōsis* (ehPIGnohsis) the recognition and full discernment, of Jesus.

> Grace and peace be multiplied unto you through the knowledge of God, and of Jesus our Lord, According as

> his divine power hath given unto us all things that pertain unto life and godliness, through the knowledge of him that hath called us to glory and virtue: Whereby are given unto us exceeding great and precious promises: that by these ye might be partakers of the divine nature, having escaped the corruption that is in the world through lust.

Knowledge and faith release the new life inside us. It enables us to live our lives from the inside out, being led by the Spirit and allowing Him to control our mind, our words, our emotions and our will. By submitting to God we are able to resist Satan.

Christians expect to see an outward change after becoming born again. But the greatest change is internal as they learn what it means to be "in Christ" and "in Him" as the Bible states in the New Testament. This position of being in Christ produces *in us* a confident expectation which is the biblical definition of hope.

In Romans 5 we are reminded that if God died for us when we were sinners and didn't know what He was doing, how much more will He rescue us when we choose to receive Him. Sufferings may come to us through an attack on our mind and body or from others and their systems based on the kingdom of darkness, but we can rejoice because when we take our stand of trust in Him and His promises, we grow stronger and may confidently expect His victory in our life.

The Purpose of Being Born Again

Salvation is not automatic as some are hoping, however. It is not limited to certain people as some teach either. John 3:16 the hallmark verse most people have heard was spoken to one of the most religious men in Jerusalem in Jesus' day. It is still the heavenly kingdom standard for mankind.

Jesus boldly and unapologetically declared to Nicodemus, "For God so loved the world, that he gave his only begotten Son, that whosoever believeth in him should not perish, but have everlasting life." Whosoever means exactly what it says. Anyone who wants to come to Jesus can be saved.

But they must make a decision to believe. The word for believe is *pisteuō* (pisSTOOoh) which means putting your belief in or trust in. The importance is realizing this is not a belief that God exists or Jesus lived. It is placing your belief and trust in Him. This means in His work for you through His death and resurrection which redeemed you from the curse of the law.

The person who acknowledges that Jesus lived but denies His resurrection does not have everlasting life. The person who believes Jesus lived, that He may have risen from the dead but insists that He is not God, doesn't have everlasting life. Neither does the person who has determined the cross isn't necessary. None of these "believers" know, *ginōskō*, God.

John 3:17 and 18 may not be so well known:

> For God sent not his Son into the world to condemn the world; but

> that the world through him might be saved. He that believeth on him is not condemned: but he that believeth not is condemned already, because he hath not believed in the name of the only begotten Son of God.

Notice that the person who doesn't put his trust in Jesus is already condemned because of Adam's disobedience and fallen nature. In essence they are without help and left to themselves if they refuse to be born again. Not later. Now.

Technically, refusing Jesus is not why they are condemned. It is the reason they remain separated/condemned. Jesus wasn't sent to condemn or punish us but to set us free from the dominion of darkness.

There are some who believe in God or a god and think the way to be saved is through their behavior. We call this works. But it is really behavior modification. You know what you are supposed to do so you change your behavior to fit the standard.

That was how the law was supposed to work in theory, but it couldn't bring the spiritual change needed to obey it. We need an internal transformation; that was the lesson the law taught. Spiritual change only comes about through faith in Jesus and His indwelling Spirit.

Sin separated us from God and drove us from His presence. In the Jewish Temple, a veil separated the place called the Holy of Holies where God's presence dwelt. On the day Jesus died on the cross, at the very moment, the veil tore, opening the way to God. When He declared, "It is finished," sin and death were defeated and the veil tore before He rose from the dead.

Many believers think it doesn't matter what name you give God because all gods are the same. The Bible does not teach that. It says there is only one name by which you are saved. That name is Jesus. "Neither is there salvation in any other: for there is none other name under heaven given among men, whereby we must be saved." (Acts 4:12)

There is no third option for man presented in the Bible. Man can never be his own boss. He was given authority; he didn't generate it from himself. He was created to have a lord. There is only God and Satan. Life and death. Blessings and curses. Salvation and hell. The idea that man can succeed on his own is a flawed image of what man is and what is possible for him.

Since the Garden, Satan has twisted God's words and copied God's principles. He has to because he can't create different rules. But one of his best ploys is to deceive man into thinking he governs himself, and it is uneducated to think a devil exists or the Bible is factual. This type of thinking blames God for all that is wrong with the world, and is blind to the truth.

People have faith. There are over four thousand religions in the world with 84% of the world's population affiliated with one. Faith is not the problem. What you believe to be true about God determines if you have a set of beliefs that have changed your habits but not your sin state, otherwise known as religion, or a trust that has transformed your life to the core of your being, recreated your spirit and cleansed you from sin.

Jesus is the only Son of God and the only one who was crucified specifically to pay for the world's sin. He is also the only one to rise from the dead and visibly ascend to heaven as five hundred witnesses could testify. (1Corinthians 15) He is the only God who can legitimately forgive sin and remove your fallen nature.

Some think being baptized in water is your entry into God's kingdom. That is not supported by the Bible either. Baptism is an outward testimony of your decision to be born from above. It is performed after you trust in Jesus, but it alone is not what saves you.

The true salvation experience is a transformation in the life of a believer, the new creation we talked about. It only comes through the blood of Jesus and trusting in Him.

Which brings us to the topic we've been kicking down the road for the last five chapters. You might wonder why God chose blood to be the covering or the way to forgiveness, animal blood in the Old Testament, and Jesus' blood for the New Covenant.

Blood as a way to forgiveness or atonement began in Genesis 3:21. Adam and Eve may have been shocked that God killed an innocent animal and made skins to cover them. Next we see Abel bringing a sheep as a sacrifice to God, and the idea that blood covered a wrong, or sin as it came to be called, followed.

Many think animal sacrifice was a pagan rite, but

The Purpose of Being Born Again

the Bible reveals a different story. It began with believers and became corrupted by unbelievers. Eventually animal sacrifices were used to honor idols. God never commanded or endorsed human sacrifices as a form of Israelite worship.

Some refer to Jesus' death as God requiring human sacrifice. Actually since Jesus is God,[1] it is more like a suicide say others. Except it isn't. This is speaking only with the silly reasonings of skeptics.

Jesus' death and resurrection was a sovereign sacrifice for the purpose of our salvation and merciful rescue from an evil foe. God did for us what we could not do for ourselves and what couldn't be done any other way.

In the book of Exodus, animal blood sacrifice is prevalent as the only way to be rescued. Fasting was important, so was prayer and good works, but blood was the only rescue when you screwed up. If you remove the blood sacrifices of the Old Testament, you remove forgiveness.

God said life is in the blood. He used it for the purpose of forgiveness. "For the life of the flesh is in the blood: and I have given it to you upon the altar to make an atonement for your souls: for it is the blood that maketh an atonement for the soul." (Leviticus 17:11) This is echoed in Hebrews 9:22 which says without the shedding of blood there was no pardoning of sins.

Now you can understand why Jesus chased the

---

[1] You can read *Is Jesus God?* by Flying Eagle Publications to find out more about Jesus' deity.

market out of the Temple court of the Gentiles in Jerusalem. The priests were disrespecting and preventing the Gentile's right to forgiveness.

Jesus as God had the purest blood over any animal or any other man. It is why after He died on the cross no other sacrifice was needed. He did what no one else could do, and He did it because He loves people.

He wants them—and you— to be free of the law of sin and death and its curses. It is just a matter of receiving what He has already done for you. But God allows you to choose your destiny, both on earth and in heaven because they are connected. The moment you decide what you believe about God, you set the course of your life.

Dying is not ceasing to exist, and the fear of death is real for the person who is not born again. It is entering into the future you have determined for yourself based on your choice of your lord. Many people say they will only live once so they aim to do what they can. But for the one who chooses Jesus as their Lord, they will only die once and live forever. For those who reject God and choose Satan, knowingly or unknowingly, they will live once and languish in torment forever.

Hebrews 9:27 says it is appointed once for a man to die. This doesn't mean a specific date because the Bible is also clear there are things you do that may lengthen or shorten your life. These things have nothing to do with eating chips and donuts but how you honor God. There are two ways man lives apart from God according to Ephesians 2:3, in the flesh and in the mind.

The Purpose of Being Born Again

Perhaps you thought reading about the covenants had nothing to do with being born again. But they too are connected. They are like legal contracts showing you what you may expect based on your choices.

Jesus described His identity and crucifixion to Nicodemus. The priest had come curious and Jesus kindly revealed Himself to him. Jesus said:

> And no one has ascended up to Heaven except He who came down from Heaven, the Son of Man who is in Heaven. But even as Moses lifted up the serpent in the wilderness, even so must the Son of Man be lifted up, so that whosoever believes in Him should not perish, but have everlasting life.
> John 13-15(MKJV)

Nicodemus recognized the Old Testament reference to the Son of Man. He knew the story of Moses lifting up a bronze snake to save the Israelites from death for their sin. But he would not understand their full meanings pointing to the new life Jesus was bringing to the world through His death and resurrection until after he received this new life for himself.

There are many books about being born again, including this little one. But none compare to the ultimate guide which is the book of Romans.

Now we know that everything in the

Law applies to those who live under the Law, in order to stop all human excuses and bring the whole world under God's judgment. For no one is put right in God's sight by doing what the Law requires; what the Law does is to make us know that we have sinned. But now God's way of putting people right with himself has been revealed. It has nothing to do with law, even though the Law of Moses and the prophets gave their witness to it. God puts people right through their faith in Jesus Christ. God does this to all who believe in Christ, because there is no difference at all: everyone has sinned and is far away from God's saving presence. But by the free gift of God's grace all are put right with him through Christ Jesus, who sets them free. God offered him, so that by his blood he should become the means by which people's sins are forgiven through their faith in him.

Romans 3:19-25 GNB

Doing good works won't save you. Keeping a list of rules won't save you. You are already a sinner and have a fallen nature as we've learned. The only way to be saved from a life lived under the authority of darkness and separated from God is to trust in Jesus' death on the cross that put all of sin and all that's contained in the curse on the God who loves you, who came to do what you couldn't do for yourself.

He wants you to know Him and to live in this love forever. That is eternal life and the purpose for being born again.

Going Deeper

Explain how being born again helps you while you live on the earth.

What is everlasting life?

What do you know about God?

Are these things the same as knowing Him? Why or why not?

Describe a true believer.

What releases this new life within us?

What is the New Testament definition of believe?

Why did God use blood as a way to forgive sin?

If anyone can be saved, why are some people condemned to live out their eternity in hell separated from God?

What is the purpose of being born again?

Take time to submit to God. Ask Him how to have a closer relationship with Him. Commit to do what He tells you.

Chapter 7

How to be Born Again

Did you know Jesus existed from the beginning? It was through Him God created the world. (John 1:1-3) Jesus had to become a man on earth to be a legal entity to use the free will and dominion given to man and become the perfect sacrifice. But His Father was perfect because His Father was God. His mother was a virgin. She became pregnant when she accepted God's word. And then the Word became flesh as John told us.

Jesus never sinned. He lived the only perfect life, and He is the only one who could serve as our Deliverer. He began His ministry when He was thirty, the age Jewish priests began their duties. Later, He surrendered His life to those wanting to crucify Him.

He died on the cross with all the world's sin upon Him. Like the sacrificial lambs of the Jewish religion, He died to cleanse people of their sins. Three days later He rose from the dead, showing His victory over death. Afterwards, He returned to Heaven and sent His Spirit into the earth.

Your sins have already been paid for, but you need to apply that work to your life. Your repentance isn't motivating God to forgive you; He did that 2,000 years ago. He's waiting for you to receive the forgiveness He provided. You must use your free will to choose Him. He will not make the decision for you.

This is why Jesus told Nicodemus "whosoever." His offer of salvation is to those who believe in Him. Jesus said, "For God so loved the world, that he gave his only begotten Son, that whosoever believeth in him should not perish, but have everlasting life." The only barrier to salvation is you. Will you accept Him?

Contrary to what most people believe, there are not different ways to get to heaven. It matters what you believe and in whom. Jesus said of Himself,"I am the way, the truth, and the life: no man cometh unto the Father, but by me." (John 14:6) Speaking of Jesus Act 4:12 says, "Neither is there salvation in any other: for there is none other name under heaven given among men, whereby we must be saved."

Hopefully by now you understand these other gods are Satan and his fallen angels. But you don't have to go on spiritual quest to find God. You don't have to perform feats of spiritual greatness to get His attention. God has made it so easy to get to Him that His way is scorned. Romans 10:6-10 says :

> But the righteousness which is of faith says this, "Don't say in your heart, 'Who will ascend into heaven?' (that

> is, to bring Christ down); or, 'Who will descend into the abyss?' (that is, to bring Christ up from the dead.)" But what does it say? "The word is near you, in your mouth, and in your heart;" that is, the word of faith, which we preach: that if you will confess with your mouth that Jesus is Lord, and believe in your heart that God raised him from the dead, you will be saved. For with the heart, one believes unto righteousness; and with the mouth confession is made unto salvation. (WEB)

God's way is you believe in your heart and say it with your mouth. God isn't controlling every detail of life. It is up to you to receive what He has freely given out of joy, love and goodwill towards us. You do that by believing Jesus is Lord and that God raised Him from the dead. Then you confess it.

If you would like to be born from above and enter into fellowship with Him and become a citizen of the kingdom of God with its unique government and benefits, here is a sample prayer:

> *Father God, I come to You believing that You sent your Son Jesus to die on the cross for me. I believe Jesus is Lord, that He died and rose again and He paid for my sins. I am sorry for all the wrong things I've*

> done, and I ask for Your forgiveness. I ask that you come into my heart, fill me with Your Holy Spirit and help me to live for You everyday of my life. Thank You, Father for this new life You have given me. In Jesus name, Amen.

Let's assume you had the good sense to pray that prayer. You have come alive (John 14:18-19 TPT; Ephesians 2:5 NIV), and Jesus is living in your heart. Put your trust in Him that it is done. Start reading the Bible and doing what it says.

New believers have a lot to learn, so here are some pointers. Jesus said if you love Him you will obey Him. The Bible says people will know us by our fruit, what we do and produce in our life. When we produce good fruit, actions and reactions, then people will know we belong to God. They need to witness your transformed life.

But as we've said, obedience isn't what enables you to be saved. Obedience enables you to live in the fullness of your blessing. Disobedience causes Satan to gain territory in your mind. You don't want him there to do his dirty work creating confusion and chaos.

Many believers want Jesus as their Savior but not their Lord. It is crucial to live submitted in your spirit to God and giving His word first place in your life. It is His word over your matter, whatever the matter is. This is part of working out your salvation; you are putting it into practice. (Philippians 2:12-13)

How to be Born Again

If you refuse to make Jesus your Lord, you disregard His counsel and direction for your life. You are willing enough to be saved but are concentrating on doing life your way through your will, thoughts and emotions. This way is hard. Also if you are unwilling to surrender to God, you may not be born again because you don't want to know, *ginōskō*, Him.

God has given us a conscience, and it helps us know if we get off track because we lose our peace if the Holy Spirit alerts it to a problem. When that happens or you knowingly do something that is sin, you ask God to forgive you, forgive anyone you are upset with, and your peace will return.

If sinning doesn't make you feel uneasy in your conscience, you are either ignorant of what the Bible says in that area or have not been transformed in your spirit. Some who think they have lost their salvation never owned it. A born again person may sin, but they will not make it their goal. (1John 3:9)

It is possible to taste Christianity but never swallow. You do this by attending church, even reading the Bible and keeping rules. But you do not have the deep love relationship of knowing God.

God wants us to stay in perfect peace with Him. Repentance keeps us in an attitude of humility and teachableness. Cain didn't have this attitude, and even though he believed in God, he hardened himself against correction. (Genesis 4)

Repent means to change your mind for the better. For example, if you are stealing from your employer, you use your spirit to tell your mind and your mouth to inform your will you aren't going to do that anymore according to God's word, and you are going to submit to the Holy Spirit in that area. You can strengthen yourself by confessing God's word on the subject and speaking in tongues concerning the issue.[1]

Some believers after receiving their salvation by God's free favor slip into legalism which is thinking that obedience makes you right with God. Or, they return to sinning and their old way of living, thinking God's grace covers whatever they do anyway. Both are extremes, and both can make you miss the fullness of God's will for you.

If you focus on loving God, reading His word then putting it into practice and being sensitive to His voice, you will end up living a life that is worthy of Him. (Colossians 1:10) Remember, if God died for you before you accepted Him, He is more than willing to help you, heal you and provide for you after you accept Him. "Now we have received, not the spirit of the world, but the spirit which is of God; that we might know the things that are freely given to us of God." (1Cor 2:12)

You must remember it is your spirit that is born again when you receive Jesus. *Your mind needs to be renewed.* Romans 12:2 says, "And be not conformed to this world: but be ye transformed by the renewing of your mind..." You renew your mind, specifically the way you think and speak, by reading God's word and

---

[1] Speaking in tongues is a product of being baptized in the Holy Spirit.

thinking on it. Your success on earth as a Christian depends upon it.

Remember too, you are living from your spirit now. You can tell your mind what it can think. You can tell your body that it is healed by Jesus' stripes. (1Peter 2:24) You can submit to God and resist Satan. Find a spirit-filled church where you can attend with other believers. It will help you form relationships with others who can encourage you.

Nicodemus must have believed Jesus and pondered His words because he spoke up for Him later in John 7:50-51. He came out into the open to help prepare Jesus' body for burial, providing almost a hundred pounds of spices for the ritual himself. It seems his trust and love for Jesus had increased to the point he no longer feared his fellow priests or the threat of being kicked out of the Jewish religious society.

We hear no more of Nicodemus after Jesus' death. We do not know if he stayed in Jerusalem or how long he lived, but it is most likely he was one of the early Christians.

Let's review. We have learned that mankind is born into a fallen state because of Adam's rebellion against God. But God in His mercy and through His goodwill towards us provided a way for us to be saved from the dominion of darkness and brought back into fellowship with Him.

That way was through Jesus' death and resurrection. It is man's choice to receive or reject God's way of salvation. If you receive it, He gives you a new spirit and you live free from the curse of the law. Romans 8:1-2 says, "There is therefore now no condemnation to those in Christ Jesus, who do not walk according to flesh, but according to Spirit. For the Law of the Spirit of life in Christ Jesus set me free from the law of sin and of death."

A born again person is free in Jesus. Free to live in abundant love. Free to have a peace that goes beyond our understanding. Free to have an intimate relationship with the Creator of your life. Free to live a healthy, prosperous life.

You are that person if you prayed to receive Jesus. Congratulations. You are on the path of abundant life. Now it is time for you to share this Good News with others.

Thank you for purchasing *Born Again Not Just For Heaven*. We hope it has been a blessing to you. If you found the book useful, please consider leaving a review online. For more titles and extras, visit our website flyingeaglepublications.com.

Going Deeper

Who does the Bible say may be saved?

Why does it matter what and in whom you believe concerning religions?

When did Jesus pay for the forgiveness of your sins? How do you access this forgiveness?

Explain the difference between receiving Jesus as your Savior and making Him the Lord of your life.

Why is obedience important?

Is it wise to be led by your soul? Why or why not?

Why should you make the effort to renew your mind and how do you do it?

Describe man's triune nature again and explain how to live inside out.

Review what you've learned about being born again. How will you apply this knowledge to yourself?

Spend time praising God for revealing this information to you, and thank Him for helping you add to your understanding as you read His word in the Bible.

Bibliography

Bareket, Elinoar. "Chesed: A Reciprocal Covenant." *The Torah.com*. 2017. https://www.thetorah.com/article/chesed-a-reciprocal-covenant

Barna. "How We Got Here: Spiritual and Political Profiles of America." Barna. May 23, 2017. https://www.barna.com/research/got-spiritual-political-profiles-america/

Barna, George. "Where Born Agains Are Missing The Mark." George Barna. May 24, 2017. https://www.georgebarna.com/research-flow/2017/5/24/where-born-agains-are-missing-the-mark

Sabin, Lamiat. "Why You're Almost Certainly More Like Your Father Than Your Mother." *Independent*, March 4, 2015.

Smietana, Bob. "Many Who Call Themselves Evangelical Don't Actually Hold Evangelical Beliefs." LifeWay Research. December 6, 2017. https://lifewayresearch.com/2017/12/06/many-evangelicals-dont-hold-evangelical-beliefs/

Strong, James. *Strong's Exhaustive Concordance of the Bible*. Abingdon Press, 1890. Online versions available.

Thayer, Joseph H. *The New Thayer's Greek-English Lexicon of the New Testament*. Peabody, MA: Hendrickson, 1981. (Online version available at https://www.studylight.org/lexicons/)

VerBrugge, Verlyn D. *New International Dictionary of New Testament Theology: Abridged Edition*. Grand Rapids, MI: Zondervan, 2000.

Weber, Jeremy. "Evangelical vs. Born Again: A Survey of What Americans Say and Believe Beyond Politics." *Christianity Today*, December 6, 2017. https://www.christianitytoday.com/news/2017/december/you-must-be-born-again-evangelical-beliefs-politics-survey.html

Zylstra, Sarah Eekhoff. "1 in 3 American Evangelicals Is a Person of Color."*Christianity Today*, September 6, 2017. https://www.christianitytoday.com/news/2017/september/1-in-3-american-evangelicals-person-of-color-prri-atlas.html

www.ingramcontent.com/pod-product-compliance
Lightning Source LLC
Chambersburg PA
CBHW071400080526
44587CB00017B/3148